CHOOSING YOUR WAY THROUGH AMERICA'S PAST

BOOK 4

ADVENTURES

from 1900 - 1920's

Anne E. Schraff

illustrated by Steven Meyers

WALCH PUBLISHING

Cover art: © North Wind Picture Archives
Marching on to Suffrage, May 6, 1911 5th Ave., New York City

Background: © Erwin Raisz, Landforms of the United States

1   2   3   4   5   6   7   8   9   10

ISBN 0-8251-2617-7

Copyright © 1990, 1991
J. Weston Walch, Publisher
P. O. Box 658 • Portland, Maine 04104-0658

Printed in the United States of America

Contents

Introduction

Most history books focus on famous people and reveal little about what the average person was doing at the time. This book highlights the courage, determination, and plain hard work of ordinary people, and it does so in an unusual way with adventures you participate in. Each adventure casts you as the central character and, at critical junctures, requires you to choose between options. Based on two sets of choices, each adventure has four possible outcomes—some tragic, some triumphant, just as they were for the real people of the times.

Your role is fictional, but the historical details are accurate. Each story is supplemented by a short passage containing interesting facts related to the period, a true/false or matching quiz, and two sets of suggested activities.

Other recommended activities include:

- Reviewing vocabulary before you read each story.

- Keeping a written record of your choices and the consequences of those choices.

- Discussing alternatives with others who chose different courses of action.

- Considering whether the protagonist is male or female. (In the majority of cases, the protagonist is sex-neutral.)

- Analyzing any effects this book has had on the way you make decisions and take risks.

- Writing a report on why it would, or would not, have been fun to live during this period of American history.

This book is intended for enjoyment as well as instruction. We hope that you will find it fun.

ELLIS ISLAND DECISION

It's 1905 and you have come to America from Calabria, Italy. Before you left Italy, you had many misfortunes. Your parents died of cholera in 1887. You went to live with an aunt. She had children of her own. There was never enough food to go around. Mostly you ate just bread soaked in oil. The drought made things worse. The soil turned to stone. The heavy rains came and turned your land into a swamp. Mosquitoes swarmed.

Now, as you near Ellis Island, you are afraid. This is where the immigrants are checked to see if they are fit to enter America. What if they find fault with you? Where will you go then?

As you ride in on a barge, you see the Statue of Liberty in the mist. Your heart pounds. It is as if she is welcoming you personally to America!

You are quickly marched down to the landing dock. There are so many others! You feel like an animal in a herd. Then you are led up the stairs to a big room. Babies are crying. Every kind of person is here. Apron-wearing women with bright kerchiefs mill around. Bearded men in fur hats and peasant boots are crowded in with people carrying battered suitcases and blanket bags.

You enter the medical area. The doctor watches to see if you limp. You try to walk very straight. Then he looks for skin infections. Thankfully, you have none.

"Where are you from?" you are asked.

"Calabria, Italy," you say.

"What ocean did you cross?" you are asked.

"The Atlantic," you say. The man asks these questions to see if you have a normal mind. If you were mentally weak, they would turn you away.

Now a chalk mark is made on the coat of a woman beside you. The doctors have found an illness. She begins to cry. How sorry you feel for her.

Your eyes are checked next. Still no chalk mark on your coat. Thank Heaven!

You wait on a wooden bench until your name is called. You are asked more questions: Have you broken any laws? Are you a troublemaker? Do you have enough money to get by on until you have a job?

Then you are approved! You get a landing card. Now you must decide if you want to stay in Little Italy in New York, where a second cousin lives. Or should you go to Boston? Some of your friends from Calabria have gone there.

WWWWWWWWWWWWWWWWWWWWWWWWWWWWWWWWWWWWWWW

■ *If you stay in New York, turn to page 3.*

■ *If you go to Boston, turn to page 4.*

Find out what your fate is!

1

You are led from the building to outside walks enclosed with wire. The gates are open. You see smiling faces outside the fence. Some wave to you. They are Italians too, but you don't know them. Still, you wave back. You are so happy to be accepted into America!

You board the ferry to the Battery (the southern tip of Manhattan Island in New York). You hurry to the apartment of your second cousin in Little Italy the minute the ferry lands.

"You must see the *padrone* [labor boss]," your cousin says. "He will find you work."

The next day you meet the *padrone*. He explains that there is a need for workers in the ready-made-clothing business. "Men, women, children are all needed. Every pair of hands I can send is given work."

You nod. You will do any kind of work to get started.

The next day you arrive at the address the *padrone* gave you. It's a small room with no windows. The lighting is bad too. Men and women sit at benches and make coats from ready-cut cloth.

"You get paid by the piece," the boss explains. "So work as fast as you can."

You work fourteen hours a day and earn very little money. Your boss is very harsh. When you make a mistake, he threatens to fire you. This fills you with terror.

The floor of the shop is covered with trash and leftover cloth. You are sixteen years old, but many working here are only fourteen. You work seventy-two hours the first week. You earn only four dollars.

"So how is the *giobba* [job]?" asks your cousin.

"Not so good," you admit. "My back aches and I make so little money."

"You want to come in the bakery shop and work with me? It's hard work too. But maybe you would make more money," says your cousin.

You are not sure what kind of a boss your cousin would be. What if you are no good at the work? You don't want to ruin your cousin's business.

■ *If you stay at the ready-made-clothing work, turn to page 5.*

■ *If you go to work for your cousin, turn to page 6.*

You go down the far stairs to the railroad ticket booths. They are selling twenty-five tickets a minute. You buy a ticket to Boston.

While you wait for your train, you buy a pint of milk for a nickel. For another nickel you get a loaf of bread. A pound of cheese costs twenty cents. You now have lunch. (And some left over!) Your first meal in America.

The train is here quickly. You go aboard with a lot of fellow Italians bound for Boston. You arrive in Boston's North End. You find your way to a boarding house where your friends stayed before you. They wrote directions to the place in a letter.

"I am looking for office work in Boston," you tell the boarding-house lady.

She laughs and says, "See the *padrone* [labor boss]. He will find you some dirty low-pay job. He will call it *buona paga* [good pay]. But it will be a dollar and a quarter a day, and the *padrone* takes fifty cents!"

The *padrone* gets you a job in a restaurant. You spend all day in the hot kitchen washing pots and pans. You scour them until they shine.

"Dirty pans make the food taste bad," says the boss if he finds the tiniest smudge burned on the pan.

Well-dressed people come into the restaurant to eat. You see them in the dining room, but you never get out of the kitchen. You must eat your hurried meals in the kitchen. Sometimes a handsome young tenor sings *O Sole Mio* out in the dining room. But the sound of your pots and pans scraping together drowns out the music in the kitchen. The music only makes you homesick.

"Do not complain," a boy at the boarding house tells you. "Look at me. All day I chop the ground with the pick and shovel. I make big holes. My arms and my back are so sore they feel like they are not a part of me."

Maybe you made a mistake coming to Boston. Back in Italy you lived on a farm. It was not your land. You were only a worker on the landlord's farm. But you learned something about farming. Maybe now if you found some friends with a little money, you could all buy a farm. How nice it would be to raise big juicy tomatoes!

■ *If you try to farm, turn to page 7.*

■ *If you stay where you are, turn to page 8.*

You remain at work in the ready-made shop. Then you get a job at another place. You now are quite good at this work. You can make better money. You work on the eighth floor of a ten-story building. Your job is making shirtwaists (women's blouses).

On a Saturday afternoon in March of 1911, you smell smoke at work. You turn to a nineteen-year-old Jewish immigrant who works beside you. "What is that? Where is it coming from?"

"Maybe somebody dropped ashes in some old rags," says your co-worker. Almost all the workers here are Italian or Jewish immigrants between the ages of thirteen and twenty-three. "They say this building is fireproof. So we have nothing to worry about."

But within minutes the smoke grows thicker. It burns your eyes. You and the others hurry toward the doors. But the first door you reach is locked! You run to the windows. But you are a hundred feet up from the sidewalk!

Everybody grows panicky. There is a lot of pushing and shoving. Flames are licking at the piles of debris on the floor. The fabric is burning very quickly. Outside, men are trying to put out the fire with pails of water. But the flames are leaping ever higher!

At last you find an unlocked door. You rush through to the fire escape. You jump onto it. But as you hurry down, you see that the fire escape ends twelve feet above a skylight (a window in the roof of another building). You must turn around and find another way to escape.

You must climb up the fire escape to the roof. Others are doing the same thing.

The fire is now raging through the eighth floor. It sweeps up to the ninth and tenth floors quickly. You hear fire engines wailing in the streets below. But they cannot reach all of you who are trapped on the roof. The longest fire equipment is too short for such a tall building.

The firemen hoist up their ladders. The lucky people on the lower floors are rescued. But you are beyond help!

"We are doomed!" screams a companion.

"Look!" you cry. "The firemen have safety nets. They want us to jump. We must jump!"

"Never," your companion groans. "Those nets will never hold people jumping so far. We will crash through."

"Better that than to burn to death," you answer.

You jump. But you crash through the safety net like a stone. You die on the pavement below. This terrible fire at the Triangle Shirtwaist Company will claim 146 young lives.

■ *Turn to page 9.*

You join your cousin in the bakery shop. It is only a hole squeezed between the barber shop and the grocery. But then the grocery closes. You turn the bakery into a small Italian restaurant. You make pasta, noodles, and macaroni. You cook veal in olive oil and put on special sauces. You must work seven days a week, twelve hours a day. And your cousin is no angel to work for. You get yelled at a lot of times. But every day you learn more.

Soon you are a fine baker. Your specialty is dessert. You make a raised bread roll filled with raisins, citron, nuts, and cherries. You get a lot of compliments.

Business is very good. You have a few tables where people can sit down. They are always full. Many others take out food to eat at home.

You grow to love Little Italy. It's a wonderful place. You love the pretty markets and the vendors who hawk their products in rich tenor voices. When you are not working in the restaurant, you visit the candle and statue shops.

On the feast of Our Lady of Mount Carmel there's a big celebration. You walk barefoot in a procession led by the Italian priest. There are so many flowers and songs! The streets dance with bright lights. The music is all around you like sweet thunder. And then you eat a big, wonderful dinner.

Not only Italian people come to your restaurant. Greeks and Syrians also come. How big and swarthy (dark) they are, and so full of laughter. You like them. You like the Poles and Germans, Jews with long beards, and Turks too. Some black men and women come just to buy your sweet bread.

After you are married, you remain in Little Italy. It is home now. You write letters to relatives back in Calabria. But you never think of going back, except for a visit.

When young relatives come to America later, you enjoy telling them about your struggles. Over and over you talk about how scared you were at Ellis Island. "But now I am an American," you say with great pride. "And the struggle was worthwhile."

■ *Turn to page 9.*

You meet someone from Calabria and get married. You borrow a little money and go with another young couple to a small town in Ohio. You buy a run-down farm and begin to plant your tomatoes.

In Italy you were a *contadini*, a farm laborer. You had a few farm tools, but not like American farmers have. You had a *zappa* (wide axe) and an ancient wooden plow.

Your German neighbors smile at how little you know. But they help you learn. You get chickens and a cow and then start your crop.

One day, after the tomatoes are already little dark green plants, you admire them. "Look," you say to your spouse. "See the little yellow blossoms? Those will be the tomatoes."

"So many yellow flowers!" cries your spouse happily.

Soon there are tiny green tomatoes all over your plants. They turn pale and yellowish and then they are red. But then monster-sized bugs appear on your precious tomatoes. "We are ruined!" you scream. You never saw such big, horrible bugs before in your life!

You and your spouse are wringing your hands when the German neighbor comes over. "What disaster has struck?" he asks.

"Look! A terrible horde of monster bugs are eating our tomatoes!" you cry.

The German farmer laughs. "No, no. The tomato hornworm is an ugly fellow. But you can defeat him. Just knock him off the plants!"

When you learn to outwit the hornworm, you get a good tomato crop.

But you never really like the farm. You don't enjoy farming the way your German neighbors do. You sell your tomatoes to an Italian who makes tomato sauce. Then you sell the farm and go to work for the company making the sauce. It turns out that you like making sauce better than you liked growing tomatoes.

You and your spouse move into Little Italy in Cleveland, Ohio. The sights and sounds of the Italian neighborhood cheer both of you. You like living in a city again. This is where you belong.

■ *Turn to page 9.*

You stay at the restaurant until one rainy day in December. You drop a heavy frying pan on your boss's foot!

"Get out, stupid!" he screams at you. You are without a job as you see the rain turn to snow. You have enough money to stay at the boarding house for another week. If you have no job by then, you are out in the street.

You are very scared. You wish you had stayed in Calabria. At least you had close family there. They would not have let you starve. You would not have died in the street of the cold. And such cold it is! You never felt such bone-chilling cold.

You go to the small, frame Italian church. You wake up the priest. You are so ashamed to be begging. But he is very nice. He gives you a hot cup of coffee and says, "You must join the mutual-aid society. It's a wonderful thing for Italians. You have sick benefits, and if you die the family is paid a thousand dollars." He smiles and gives you five dollars from the poor box and the address of the mutual-aid society.

You go to the mutual-aid society. They find you a new job in a clothing store. You feel so much better. It is like having a family again.

You are sick for several days. While you are sick, the members of the society visit you. One especially nice older woman visits you every day.

"I will bring you something good to eat. What do you feel like?" she asks.

"Chocolate ice cream," you say.

She returns in the afternoon with chocolate ice cream. "Ah! You look much better," she says.

"I feel better," you say.

"We mutual-aid members never forget our own," the lady says. "When you had the high fever, I thought you would maybe die. If such a thing had happened, we would have all come to your funeral. We sing the dead person into paradise. And we even bring a band. The musicians play for nothing."

You are glad you didn't need the musicians just now! But you never forget the mutual-aid society. You always remain a member. When you get married and are very successful, you still belong. You could not have made it in this new country without the mutual-aid society.

■ *Turn to page 9.*

The Mayor and the Funnies

Fiorello La Guardia was born in New York in 1882. His father had come from Italy and become a bandmaster in the United States Army. Young Fiorello was an aviator in World War I. Then he got into politics. He became the very popular mayor of New York in 1933. This son of an Italian immigrant built parks and low-cost houses. He built roads and even an airport in New York.

But to the children of New York the biggest thing La Guardia ever did was read the comics in the Sunday paper. There was a newspaper strike in New York. The children really missed the comics. So the mayor decided to do something about it. He read all the comic strips over the radio. This was so popular that he kept right on doing it.

Not everybody in New York liked Mayor La Guardia, but all the children loved him.

True/False

_____ 1. The first thing immigrants saw as they neared New York was the Statue of Liberty.

_____ 2. Ellis Island was used to check over immigrants.

_____ 3. Fiorello La Guardia was governor of New York.

_____ 4. Children liked La Guardia because he wrote funny comic strips.

_____ 5. A chalk mark was much feared by immigrants.

Group Activities

1. Make a large class poster of Ellis Island scenes. Look at photos in books and sketch copies. Many students should contribute their artistic skills.

2. Since America is a land of immigrants, many of our most popular foods were brought from other nations. As a class project, discover as many of these dishes with foreign origins as you can.

3. Using an encyclopedia or almanacs, look up all the Americans who won medals in the last two Olympics. Write their names and ancestries on the board. You will be surprised about the varied ethnic backgrounds you find. (Finding the ancestries might require some research in sports encyclopedias.)

Individual Activities

1. Write a paragraph about one of the following famous Italian-Americans:
   Mario Lanza   Antonin Scalia   Constantini Brumidi

2. Describe the feelings that were probably strongest in the heart of a new immigrant arriving at Ellis Island. Write a paragraph about it as if the immigrant were you.

3. Find out what Ellis Island is like today. It no longer receives immigrants. What has happened to the buildings?

MUCKRAKERS WANTED

It is 1905 and you are a young reporter. After you graduated from college you got a job at a small magazine. One day your editor calls you in.

"Well, we need two stories. I'm offering you a choice. Do you want to do a piece on the rich folks and their yachts? Or do you want to look into the meat-packing industry? Lot of shocking stuff going on there," your editor says.

You want to make a name for yourself as a reporter. You have always dreamed of being a novelist. After writing some fine articles, maybe you can turn to a great novel. It would be fun to spend some time on those beautiful yachts. But maybe you'd get a name faster if you wrote about the meat industry.

"If you want to cover the lives of the Vanderbilts and the Goulds, you can go to all those ritzy parties. And they'll take you on their yachts and to the horse races," says your editor with a wink and a grin.

It sure wouldn't hurt to have rich friends. And by spending time with them and writing about them, you could make them your friends.

But you have always admired the muckrakers. They are reporters who find something wrong and write about it. You think that muckrakers do a lot of good. One of your special heroes is Charles Dickens. He wrote all those wonderful books exposing evils. He wrote about orphans who were starved and beaten. He pointed to the misery and diseases of the poor people of England. His books moved people to do something about things that were wrong.

You would like to make a difference too. If things are wrong in the meat industry, somebody should report it. It's a threat to the health of the

country when the meat supply is not good. Perhaps you ought to go for that story.

"Well," says your editor. "What will it be? Yachting and horse racing, or the meat-packing business? It's up to you. I know you'll do a good job with whatever story you take."

//

■ *If you choose the meat-packing story,
turn to page 13.*

■ *If you choose to report on the rich people,
turn to page 14.*

Find out what your fate is!

You put aside your good clothes and dress in a shabby coat. You don't want to stand out when you go to the Chicago stockyards.

Before you see your assignment, you *smell* it. There's a strong odor as you near the stockyards. You are not used to it. It makes you sick. The people who ride the trolley with you don't seem to notice it. Maybe you get used to such an awful smell!

When you get inside the stockyards, you see more cows than you thought lived on earth. So many cows! You see hogs and sheep too. Such a noise they are making!

You never lived on a farm. This is all new to you. You don't like it much. You eat beef and lamb. But you never thought much about it being cows and sheep!

Suddenly you think maybe you'll become a vegetarian (someone who doesn't eat meat)!

You fear you made a mistake coming here. You feel sorry for all the animals. You feel sorry for the workers too. They are mostly immigrants. The ones you see are Polish and Lithuanian. They don't understand what the bosses say to them.

"Oh!" you gasp as a horrible accident happens before your eyes. A man's leg was just crushed by a truck coming from a hallway. It was loaded with meat. The boss told the man to keep out of the hallway. But the Polish worker did not understand the warning. Now his leg is twisted and bloody!

"Idiot!" yells the boss. "It's your own fault!"

You make a note of what you saw. How dangerous it is for bosses to give safety warnings in English to men who don't speak English!

Soon you see other things that disgust you. The filth from the stockyard is pushed into the Chicago River. The river is full of grease and chemicals! And you see beef covered with boils. It is meat from sick animals. The meat is sent to the cannery anyway. People will eat that and get sick.

You have seen enough to write a shocking magazine article. But right now a tough-looking fellow is coming toward you. "What are you snooping around for?" he demands. He sees your notebook! "Listen, if you are one of those nosy reporters, I'll break your neck! If I see any articles about this place, I'll track you down and make you sorry!"

Chills run up your spine.

■ *If your decide to write your story anyway, turn to page 15.*

■ *If not, turn to page 16.*

You are a little disappointed in yourself that you made this choice. But the thought of going into a meat-packing plant is too awful. Just the smell of such a place would make you ill! No, you just can't do it.

And it *is* exciting to find out how the very rich live. First you travel to Newport, Rhode Island, for the yacht races. And what yachts are on display! Big schooners and steam yachts are everywhere. One of them has thirteen thousand square feet of sail. And it's all billowing in the wind against a blue sky. What a sight! You have never seen anything so beautiful and thrilling.

The fresh salt air is in your face. Your hair blows in the wind. You are so glad you chose this assignment.

You go to the horse races at Jerome Park. It's lovely, rolling countryside. You arrive with a wealthy young couple in a fine carriage. They treat you like one of the family.

The most wonderful time is your last weekend. You are part of a jolly party riding to a country inn. A quartet of young men playing long brass horns greets you at the inn. You feel like royalty! At the inn you dine on pheasant and the most incredible desserts. You choose a strawberry shortcake covered with thick, rich cream. An ice sculpture in the shape of a bird sits in the center of the table. And when you finish dinner, you are offered little chocolate cherries filled with sweet, pink cream.

Your hosts are two brothers. One is a fine man who uses his money wisely. He give a lot to charity. You like him and his wife. The other fellow is less likable. And when you overhear him talking to a companion, you are shocked.

"Well, if the health department is causing you trouble, old chap," he says, "pay the snoop off."

The other man shrugs. "I've owned this apartment building for five years. I never had trouble before. Now this new inspector demands I put in fire escapes. He says my place is a firetrap. But it will cost a fortune to put in fire escapes. Are you sure I could pay the inspector off?"

The man who has been entertaining you laughs and says,"Of course. How do you think I keep them off my back? My buildings are in worse shape than yours."

You feel terrible. You have heard about corruption. You should report it. But then you will get people in trouble. Maybe that's not your job.

■ *If you report it, turn to page 17.*

■ *If not, turn to page 18.*

You have a notebook full of awful stuff. You must report it. You cannot be scared off by a thug! (Even though your heart is pounding.)

Your article tells all about the impure beef and the unsafe working conditions. You describe meat that smelled terrible being ground into sausages. It makes you sick just to remember it all. But you put it all down.

Your article makes a lot of people mad. You get nasty telephone calls. One man threatens you. But you know you did the right thing. Now the government will have to look into the problems at the stockyards. They will have to pass laws so spoiled meat can't be sold to people. They will have to make sure the stockyard workers aren't being injured and killed so often.

You are now excited about writing articles like this. You are making the world a better place. You feel like a kind of crusader. You are fighting for right and justice! You write another article about unsafe tenement buildings. Poor people are crowded together like sardines. Many of the buildings are firetraps.

Your tenement article makes even more people mad at you. But many others admire what you are doing. You are a hero to the average person. Your byline (the line giving your name as author) means the truth is being told.

"You're brave," says a friend. "I wouldn't stick my neck out the way you are."

You smile and shrug. You don't feel brave. You are just doing a job—an important job.

You never do get around to writing your novel. But you write many more articles and even some books about things you feel are wrong. Your book about how the railroad doesn't play fair with farmers wins a lot of prizes. You are called one of the great muckrakers of the twentieth century.

You are proud of all the work you have done. But the proudest moments of your life come when some new laws are passed. Because of you and others like you, the government passes laws to make the meat industry safer. The local government makes sure the tenements all have fire escapes.

You are really glad you chose that first assignment to check into the meat-packing business.

■ *Turn to page 19.*

You hurry away and try to forget what you saw at the meat-packing plant.

"It all seemed okay down there," you tell your editor. "No story there."

The editor looks hard at you. "No sick cows killed and turned into corned beef?" he asks.

"No. I didn't see any," you say.

"No hogs dying of cholera, then made into sausage?" asks the editor.

"All the animals looked healthy to me," you lie. You hope your nervousness doesn't show.

"How about filth being poured into the river?" your editor asks.

"I didn't see it," you mumble. You never felt less like a reporter than you do now. Every time you want to tell the truth you see that big, angry fellow. His hands were like hams. His arms were thick as oak tree trunks.

The editor gets up. He grates back his chair. He looks disgusted. "I gave you a choice. I said you could write a fluff piece [an article that isn't important]. I didn't say you had to do the muckraking piece. But you took it. Now you're lying about what you saw. You were either paid off or scared off. You sure aren't much of a reporter either way," he says.

You cannot speak. Your mouth is full of cotton. That's what it feels like, anyway. You don't want to be fired. So you quit.

You soon get another job with another newspaper. You write human-interest stories. You write about lost dogs and kittens getting trapped in trees. Sometimes you write about tea parties and what the people wore. It's not much fun. In fact, it's very boring after a while. But at least it's not dangerous.

You write some stories for adventure magazines too. But nothing sells. You settle down to being a human-interest reporter. You write mostly about weddings and parties. The only trouble you get in is when you misspell somebody's name. It's easy, pleasant work. But it's never very exciting.

■ *Turn to page 19.*

You must tell someone what you heard. If there's a dangerous tenement that could burn down, you must do something. So you hurry to the tenement off Mulberry Street. You must see it for yourself.

You go through dark hallways and dirty cellars. You hear the constant whir of sewing machines. The people not only live here but also work here.

The bedrooms are tiny, and dirty too. Each room has four beds. The smell is terrible. But it gets worse. You see a broken stove. Piles of cloth and rubbish are everywhere. A kerosene lamp gives a dull glow to the awful little room where a baby wails.

This is a four-story tenement, and there's no fire escape. If there were to be a fire, the people on the top floors would die.

You are shaking with anger. You think of that man eating strawberry shortcake and laughing. It's not fair! The people must hear about this outrage!

You rush down to your editor.

"Well, is the story about the rich folks about done?" he asks.

"No!" you almost shout. "I want to write a different story. You wouldn't believe what I just saw. Tenements filled with dirty, sick children. The rooms are like ovens. The windows are broken, so the landlord has nailed boards over them! The landlord won't fix anything. Even the toilets don't work. And the place is a firetrap!"

"I've never seen you so mad," your editor says.

"I'm going to write the article of my life!" you promise.

Your editor grins and says, "I knew you had good stuff in you. Go for it, kid!"

You write an article about the tenement on Mulberry Street. Then you tell about certain health department and safety inspectors who can be bought off. There's a big shakeup at city hall after that. An investigation is started. Four building and safety inspectors admit they took bribes to overlook dangerous conditions. New inspectors are put on the job. Soon there's a big change. Fire escapes are going in. Boarded-up windows are turned into real windows. Toilets are finally fixed.

You have made a difference, and you're proud!

■ *Turn to page 19.*

The conditions at the tenements are probably not as bad as you think. After all, these are nice people. Would they put others in danger? You don't think so.

You spend another day with the two brothers and their families. Now you are ready to write your story. You go back to your office and write a delightful tale. It sparkles with all the exciting adventures you have had. You capture the beauty and thrills of the yacht races. You capture the color and excitement of the horse races. You describe in detail the beautiful clothing your new friends wore. You write of the gentleman who never went out without his walking stick. You tell about the mustaches that are in fashion and the shoes topped off with spats (ankle coverings). It's great fun to describe the ladies' hats, big and grand, covered with bows and flowers.

You have just about finished your article when your editor looks in. "Terrible fire over off Mulberry," he says.

You remember the two men talking about the tenement. It was off Mulberry! Oh, no! It can't be!

"Four kids died in the fire," your editor says. "They were on the top floor. No fire escapes. The kids had to jump. Six got broken bones, but four were killed. Terrible thing. How come the city allows tenements like that without fire escapes?"

You know the answer! It's because safety inspectors are bribed!

You feel sick. You can't think of anything for days but those four children. Finally you get the courage to see if it was the tenement you heard about at the party.

Thank heaven it's a different tenement! But now you know what you must do. You have to make sure a tragedy like this doesn't happen again. The next article you write will be about safety for tenements.

No more stories about yacht races for you! You are a real reporter from now on. You are going to make a difference.

■ *Turn to page 19.*

Muckrakers and President Teddy Roosevelt

Around 1905 many writers called muckrakers were active. They wrote about things that needed correction. Many Americans read the muckrakers' articles. Then they demanded that something be done about the things the muckrakers wrote about. President Theodore Roosevelt decided to do something. He signed laws making food and drugs safer.

Teddy Roosevelt had six children. When he wasn't busy being president he loved to play with them. He would roll down hills and climb like a boy. He liked to say "Bully, bully" as he cheered people on. He was the first president to ride in a gas-powered car. He was also the first to ride in a plane.

President Roosevelt had a strong sense of fair play. And he knew it was not fair that some Americans had to eat bad food and live in unsafe houses. So he tried to do something about it. And he did.

Matching

1. A reporter who wrote about things that needed correction: _____ .

2. The fun-loving president of the United States: _____ .

3. A very rich family: _____ .

4. Author who wrote about starved and beaten orphans: _____ .

5. Things made safer by Roosevelt's law: _____ .

a) Teddy Roosevelt

b) Vanderbilt

c) muckraker

d) food and drugs

e) Dickens

Group Activities

1. President Teddy Roosevelt would always write letters to his children when he was away from home. He would illustrate the letters with simply drawn pictures. (Many of these letters are found in a little book titled *Theodore Roosevelt's Letters to His Children,* New American Library, 1964.) Write a short letter to a younger schoolmate (first- or second-grader) and illustrate it. Send a pack of letters from your class to the younger class.

2. Discuss some things wrong in your city that need correction. Do you have problems that nobody seems to be doing anything about? Write a letter about it to the editor of your newspaper from your class.

3. Discuss the word *muckraker.* Why are such people necessary?

Individual Activities

1. Choose one of the following muckrakers and write a paragraph about him or her:
   Upton Sinclair   Ida Tarbell   Lincoln Steffens

2. Find a newspaper article about a problem in your community that could be called "muckraking."

3. Today if people are trapped in a tall building during a fire, what might be a big help? Write a short story about how the people are rescued.

GETTING THE VOTE

It's 1914 and you are out walking with friends. It's a nice day in your northeastern town. Suddenly you hear a woman shouting. "Who's that?" you ask. A crowd has gathered to listen to her.

"That's some suffragette," your friend says. "She's making a speech."

"What's a suffragette?" you ask. You are eating an ice cream cone. It tastes good on a warm day.

"A woman who wants to vote," your friend says.

You stop and listen to the woman. "One half of American women are dolls! The rest are drudges. And we are all fools!" she cries.

"Boy, is she mad!" you say.

A young woman in the crowd turns to you. (She's about five years older than you are.) "Of course she's mad. Why shouldn't she be mad? We want to vote. Why should men be the only ones who can vote? It's our country too!"

You finish your ice cream cone and go home. At the dinner table you tell your parents about the suffragette.

"How sad," says your father. "A woman acting like that in public. I feel sorry for her. Such unladylike behavior!"

Your mother puts out dessert. It's chocolate cake with thick chocolate frosting. Your mother is the best cook in town. You're sure glad of that! But now she looks serious. "I don't see why women can't vote. I have never understood it."

Your father almost drops his napkin! "Surely, my dear, you would not want to get mixed up in politics! Why, it's such a dirty business. Smoke-filled rooms. Bad language. It's no place for a gentle lady like you."

Your mother smiles. "I didn't say I wanted to run for president, dear. I would just like to cast my vote as you do. I think a lot about the issues. I feel hurt when you go to vote and I can't," she says.

"My word!" your father mutters. He sips his tea. Then he says, "If women vote, life will not be the same. Women should not have to worry about such things. They should spend their time listening to music and enjoying good books."

Your mother laughs. "Oh, don't be a fuddy-duddy, dear. I can still listen to music if I want to. But it so happens that I don't want President Wilson reelected."

"You are against Wilson?" your father gasps.

"Oh, very much so," your mother says. "And I dearly wish I could vote against him!"

You don't know what to think. It seems fair that women be allowed to vote. But would it mean women would then be more interested in politics than in making chocolate cakes?

■ *You decide you are for women voting. Turn to page 23.*

■ *You decide you are against it. Turn to page 24.*

Find out what your fate is!

21

You can't see why your mother can't vote. She is pretty smart. She has told you a lot about history. She seems to understand all the issues of the day.

Some of your friends are excited about helping women get the vote. "Let's go do something about it," one of your friends suggests. "It's unfair that women aren't allowed to vote. There's a meeting about it down at the women's club. Maybe they could tell us how we could help."

"That'll be fun," you say. You hope they have good speakers. You love it when speakers yell and pound tables with their fists.

You go into the hall and see women of all ages gathered. A few men are there too. Very few. Some of the women have white hair. Some are young, with children. The children carry little signs that say, "I wish Ma could vote!"

A woman whose first name is Inez is the first speaker. She's a graduate of Vassar College. She's a lawyer. She says, "I want to improve the conditions of life for women and children. The best method is to give women the vote."

Some other women speak too. You like the gray-haired lady who screams about how men have mistreated women. She says the only way to get the vote is to picket and cause trouble. (You can imagine what your father would think of that!)

A sweet-faced old woman gets up and says, "I think we should gather signatures on petitions. When we get enough signatures, we can get Congress to pass the women's voting amendment."

"Petitions! Signatures! Nonsense!" shouts the gray-haired woman. "We have been trying to get the vote for fifty years! They have the right idea in England. Throw stones at public buildings! Make them put you in jail and then refuse to eat. They'll get scared if we do things like that here. They will have to give us the vote just to get peace!"

You want to help the cause of women's suffrage. But how? One group is planning a shouting, singing march demanding the vote. They might block the street and keep people from going to work. They might even block the door to the mayor's office. Another group is going to take petitions around. They will ask people to sign them.

■ *If you plan to join the march, turn to page 25.*

■ *If you plan to take petitions around, turn to page 26.*

Maybe Dad is right! Things are pretty good now. You wouldn't like your mother to change at all. She's pretty near perfect now. If she had to vote, then maybe she would stop making dumplings and fudge and lemon chiffon cake.

The next week your mother is putting on a white dress and a big hat. It's not Sunday. "Where are you going, Mother?" you ask.

"The suffragettes are marching for women's right to vote. I'm in the march," she says.

"Ma!" you gasp. "You never did anything like that before. Isn't it dangerous? Won't the police stop you?"

Your mother smiles. "No. We're just marching very nicely and carrying flags and signs asking for the vote. Remember, when the country isn't being run wisely, it hurts women as much as men. Our children have to go to war if the peace is lost. If the president doesn't handle the economy right, then our families go hungry. If Congress makes bad laws, we suffer as much as men. So we want to help choose the president and Congress."

Suddenly your father comes in. He looks sadly at you. "Do you see what Mother is doing? She is making herself a laughing-stock [ridiculous person]. She is shaming her whole family. Can't you talk to her? Maybe she'll listen to you," he says.

You can see your mother has made up her mind. She's a strong person. She wants to vote and that's that. But your father is so upset.

"You sure you have to go, Ma?" you ask. "The neighbors will see you and laugh. My friends from school will make fun of me."

Your mother straightens her hat. "I'm sorry if our neighbors do something so rude. I'm sorry if your friends can't understand that women have the right to fight for their rights. But I must do it." She turns then and looks right at you. "Do you know what I really wish? I wish you would come with me. It would mean so much to me if you stood by my side. Because this is really important to me," your mother says.

■ *If you go with her, turn to page 27.*

■ *If not, turn to page 28.*

You have never been in a march before. It's exciting. You gather with the others at the park. Then you begin marching. You carry a big American flag and walk on the side of the march. You feel as though you are in the Fourth of July parade.

Down the street you go. You look back and see many American flags fluttering in the breeze. It's a pretty sight. Most marchers are carrying banners saying, "Votes for Women."

The women wear big hats with satin ribbons. One lady is pushing a baby stroller.

Suddenly a woman steps from the curb and yells, "Shame on you! You women are a disgrace! Why aren't you home cooking and cleaning for your families? What a disgrace to be marching in the street like this!"

"We want women to vote," a woman in the march answers.

"I want my mom to be able to vote," you say. "She's smart. She wants to vote."

"You are all a disgrace. I bet your houses are dirty. I bet you make your children eat cold food so you can be out here marching!" the woman yells back.

A man on the other side of the street shouts, "It's not natural for women to vote! It will ruin our country."

When you get to the mayor's office, the police are all around. The newspaper reporters are there too.

"Oh, good," says a woman in a big flowered hat. "Now all this will be in the papers. That will help our cause!"

Three women sit down in front of the door to the mayor's office. A young policeman says, "Please, ladies, don't do that. People have to get in and out to see the mayor."

After some hollering and flag-waving, the women get up. Your march moves on down the street.

The next day your picture is in the paper. You are right there on the front page! You are right in front of the lady with the big hat.

"Why, darling," says your mother, "you look so brave! Oh, I am so proud of you! You are making history!"

But your father hides his face behind a book. He does not seem pleased with you at all. Still, you did what you thought was right. And you are sort of proud of that too.

■ *Turn to page 29.*

You start down the street in your neighborhood with your petition. You are nervous when you rap on the first door. A man comes and listens to your little speech. Then he slams the door in your face!

At the next house you go to, a woman listens politely and then tells you she doesn't want to vote. She closes the door gently.

At the third house, a little terrier dog comes rushing out. You decide you'd better run. Down the street you go, your petitions flying.

"Hey!" shouts a friend. "What are you doing?"

"I'm collecting signatures so my mom can vote," you explain.

Your friend helps you recover your petitions. Then he says, "I think that's a big mistake. Pa says women will never get the vote. He says it's nonsense. And if they do get the vote, Pa says women won't wash our clothes anymore."

You stare at your friend. "How come?" you ask.

"Well, Pa says if they get the vote they'll want to be on the school board. Then they'll want to be mayor. Then they'll want to be governor. Pretty soon they'll want to be president. Do you think the president has time to wash dirty socks?"

You burst out laughing. Then you say, "Want to help me get signatures?"

"Well, maybe. I got nothing better to do," your friend says.

You both go to a big walnut door. A white-haired woman answers the bell. You make your speech. Then the lady says, "Come in. I have some nice white cake and lemonade."

You go in eagerly. The woman signs your petition. She tells you all about her life as you eat white cake and drink icy cold lemonade. She fought against slavery when she was young. Then she worked for better hospitals for the mentally ill. "Now I hope to see women get the vote," she says. "I'm working hard for it."

You smile and thank her as you go.

"Hey," your friend says, "this is a good idea. I guess I'm for women getting the vote after all."

"How come?" you ask.

"Well, that woman must be real busy, and she still has time to make cake and lemonade," your friend says.

You laugh and hurry on. At the end of the day you have a lot of signatures. You are pretty proud of yourself.

■ *Turn to page 29.*

You rush out after your mother. You try not to look at your father. You hope he understands.

There are over a hundred marchers. Most are women, but there are a few men. There are some children too. Many flags blow in the wind.

A carriage comes down the street. "Get out of my way, you riffraff!" yells a burly man.

"Don't you yell at my Ma!" you shout at him.

"You got no business marching with flags," the man shouts back. He looks mean enough to drive his horses right into the line of march. "The Grand Army of the Republic has the right to march. Not uppity women."

The marchers just stand there staring at the angry man. They are really brave. You stand with them. You didn't really care if women got the vote or not before. Now you really want it.

Finally the angry carriage driver goes around the marchers. You walk on to the city hall. There you see many newspaper people. The police are there too. But there is no trouble. Everything is very orderly.

The next day there's a big newspaper story about the march. You wish they had taken your picture, but they didn't. Still, you are proud that you went along. Your mother is very pleased.

But your father seems to be very quiet. You hope he's not awfully mad at you.

One afternoon your father comes over to you. "You know," he says, "you did the right thing going with your mother the other day. You believed she was right. So you did what you thought was right. I'm proud of you for that."

"Thanks, Pa," you say.

Your father then walks over to your mother. She's busy darning socks. "You know, dear," he says, "when I helped start the labor union you stood by me. It was tough to start the union. But you were there with me. I guess I should stand by you in this women's vote thing. From now on, I will."

You smile at your parents. They don't always agree. But they always stick together when things get tough!

■ *Turn to page 29.*

You just can't do it. You don't want to be in some march with people laughing at you. Besides, your father doesn't want you to go.

So your mother goes off alone with her flags. You feel bad. When you needed Ma, she always stuck by you. Now she needed you and you let her go alone.

"I feel like I failed Ma," you tell your father.

"Well, she's being very foolish," your father says. But he looks sad too.

"I hope Ma will be okay," you say. "I hope nobody shoves her or anything."

Your father puts down his newspaper. But he doesn't say a word.

"Pa, remember when you started the labor union where you work? Remember how Ma went down and stood by your side? It was real scary, wasn't it? But Ma went and stood by your side anyway. I wish we were with her now," you say.

Your father grabs his hat. "Come on!" he says.

You and your dad run down the street. You have to run to catch up to the march. You see them up ahead. There are dozens of American flags blowing in the breeze. It's a thrilling sight.

A woman at the back of the march sees you. "Come on, join us. We can always use more marchers," she says.

Your father starts to say he only came to make sure his wife was okay. You try to say you are not really marching either. You're just looking for your mother. But the woman sticks a flag in your hand! And she gives your father a banner. And now you're in the march whether you want to be or not.

Some people jeer at you. You get red in the face. But you keep on moving. You try to see where your mother is. But she sees you first. A big smile breaks out on her face. "Oh!" she cries. "You came! You both came!"

You don't have the heart to tell her you only came to make sure she was all right. Your father grins sheepishly. He doesn't tell her either.

And the three of you march together, waving your flags and your banners. And after a while, you really *are* marching for women to get the vote. Because it's right.

■ *Turn to page 29.*

When Women Got the Vote

In 1920 the Nineteenth Amendment to the Constitution passed. This gave women the vote in America. For almost seventy years people had worked for this. Now, at last, it happened.

The first woman to be elected to the United States Congress was Jeanette Rankin. She was from Montana. When Congress voted to declare war in World War I, Jeanette Rankin voted against it. When Congress voted to declare war in World War II, she was the only one to vote against it. She just never could vote to go to war. In the 1960s she wasn't in the Congress anymore. But she was still fighting for peace.

As a girl, Jeannette Rankin worked for a woman's right to vote. She fought for other social welfare causes too. But she was best known as the member of the United States House of Representatives who never voted to go to war.

Matching

1. The 19th Amendment gave the vote to

   _____ .

2. Representative Rankin could never vote for

   _____ .

3. A woman fighting for women's right to vote was a

   _____ .

4. In 1914 the president of the United States was

   _____ .

5. The angry suffragette described women as dolls,

   drudges, and _____ .

a) war

b) women

c) fools

d) suffragette

e) Wilson

Group Activities

1. Do you think males and females vote differently? Make a ballot for each member of the class. Nobody should put her or his name on the ballot, but everyone should mark his or her ballot *M* for male or *F* for female. On each ballot the following questions should appear.
   a) The city has enough money for ten new police officers or a new park. Which would you choose? Police _____
   Park _____
   b) The city can build a new highway or improve the zoo. Which would you choose? Highway _____
   Zoo _____

c) A small island in the Pacific has been destroyed by a windstorm. Many are homeless. The people want to come to America. What do you say?

Yes, come _____

No, don't come _____

d) Should the voting age be lowered to 16?

Yes _____

No _____

Add up the votes on each issue. Did boys and girls vote differently? Discuss the results.

Individual Activities

1. Imagine you are a woman in 1914. Describe why you want to vote.

2. Make a poster for women's suffrage. Decorate it with pictures from papers and magazines, and use a catchy slogan.

3. Write a paragraph about one of these famous women in public life:
   Sandra Day O'Connor   Frances Perkins   Susan B. Anthony   Dorothea Dix

A FATEFUL VOYAGE

It's 1915 and you are a wealthy young American starting a wonderful adventure. You are going to Europe on an ocean liner! And what an ocean liner it is! She's called a floating palace. A big, gleaming ship in white and gold!

"But aren't you afraid to go to Europe with the war on?" asks your aunt. Your Auntie Peg worries too much.

"Oh, no," you say with a smile. "That war has nothing to do with a passenger ship. Who would bother us?"

"Well," your aunt says, "England is at war with Germany. And you are sailing to England on an English ship."

"So what?" you ask. "Germany won't bother a passenger ship."

You have all your bags packed. You have been dreaming of this trip for years. It's a gift from your parents on your high school graduation. Your parents can't go, but you will be traveling with good friends.

The *Lusitania* is the largest and fastest ship afloat. When you go to the main gangway you gasp at the ship's size. There's the captain welcoming everybody aboard. A lot of children are whooping it up as they run up the gangplank. You clutch your suitcase and wave goodbye to your parents. Your heart is pounding as the ship's whistle blows.

As the *Lusitania* sails from New York, you look at the Statue of Liberty. You watch until you can't see it anymore. You're really on your way now!

You rush to see your beautiful bedroom on the ship. It's rose-colored with rich dark wood. You even have your own bathroom. Then you go to the dining room and have your first meal. It's a delicious tender steak with baked potatoes, and banana cream pie for dessert. After the meal, you and your friends stroll on the wide deck.

It's a wonderul voyage. Every day is more fun than the one before. You are really sorry when you see the lighthouse on the Irish coast. Soon you will be in England and the voyage will be over.

You are going to have lunch soon, but you must return to your cabin first. As you walk on the top deck, you look out across the water.

Wait! Something dark is coming just underneath the water! It's coming fast. What is it? Are sharks that fast? Suddenly your legs turn numb. You *know* what the object is. It's a torpedo coming right at the *Lusitania*!

The torpedo strikes and there's a terrible explosion. Fire and smoke are everywhere. "Lower lifeboats! Abandon ship!" men are screaming. But should you jump on the first lifeboat or wait to see how serious this is?

■ *If you go on the first lifeboat, turn to page 33.*

■ *If you wait and see, turn to page 34.*

Find out what your fate is!

You decide to escape the ship quickly. The *Lusitania* is tipping over! It's going down!

You clamber onto a lifeboat. The ship is almost standing on its head now. You tumble over the side toward the water in the lifeboat. There are more explosions as the lifeboat bounces down. The lifeboat swings wildly from side to side. You cling onto the side with all your strength. The lifeboat just ahead of yours crashes into the water, spilling everyone out. They are crying and screaming.

Your own lifeboat hits the water hard. But nobody falls out. Water is seeping through a crack in the bottom.

"Row," someone shouts. You must get this leaky old lifeboat away from the *Lusitania*. When the *Lusitania* goes down there will be a big sucking action. It could pull nearby lifeboats down with it.

Another lifeboat lands on top of one already in the water. At least thirty people are crushed! What a horrible sight! You are numb with terror. You help row away from the *Lusitania*. There are about forty people in your lifeboat. Some are praying. Others are sobbing. You wonder—is this the end? Are you going to die? You have just begun your life! Why, oh, why didn't you listen to your worry-wart Auntie Peg?

You look back at the *Lusitania*. It's about to tip over. Can you get away in time?

"We're lost!" a woman wails. "We will all be crushed by the falling ship!"

"I'm jumping out and swimming for it!" a man cries.

Everybody is rowing the lifeboat with all their strength. But you are going too slowly. The great ocean liner is about to come down, and you fear you will be under her!

But how you dread jumping into the water. It's filled with debris. It's icy cold, and you are not a good swimmer. You will probably drown at once!

■ *If you stay with the lifeboat, turn to page 35.*

■ *If you jump out and swim, turn to page 36.*

You will not rush over the side like those panicky people. Some of the lifeboats are overturning, hurling people into the sea. You must wait to get a clearer picture of what's going on.

You hurry to your stateroom to get your life preserver. When you get there you find it gone. Somebody has already taken it!

When you reach the deck, you stand on one of the collapsible boats and wait for instructions. Thirty other people are already there.

"It's time to launch the boat!" a man shouts. He knocks out the pin. The lifeboat opens and then begins rolling down the side of the ship. It almost collides with another lifeboat also going over the side. Luckily, you do not crash together.

Your lifeboat carries sixty-five people. You drop into the water and begin moving away from the *Lusitania*. Luckily, a member of the crew is on the lifeboat. He knows how to handle it. He moves you quickly from the *Lusitania*.

You try not to look into the sea. It is filled with dead bodies! Some are women and children. Some are even babies! You never thought you would see such an awful sight. Many of the passengers were killed by explosions on the ship. Others were crushed as they tried to escape. Some have drowned already.

"Where are the rescue boats?" you wonder. The captain of the *Lusitania* must have radioed for help the minute the torpedo struck. You were so close to England. Rescue ships should be coming already.

"Look! Our lifeboat is leaking!" a young boy cries. "We'll never make it with so many people."

"Keep calm," says the crew member from the *Lusitania*. But the lifeboat is slowly filling with water. Maybe you should climb out and look for a safer lifeboat. Some are not so crowded as this one. Sixty-five people is a lot for a lifeboat that is leaking.

You glance across the water. You see people swimming. Some are hanging onto debris. Others are trying to reach lifeboats. You see a man in a lifeboat shout to a swimmer, "No room in here!"

■ *If you look for another lifeboat, turn to page 37.*

■ *If you stay in this one, turn to page 38.*

You cannot make yourself jump into the water. You help the others row faster. The *Lusitania* is creaking and groaning. You remember reading in an adventure book that a dying ship cries out like a person. It's true. You can hear the death groans of the *Lusitania*. She is standing on her bow with her stern out of the water. People are still on the deck. They are screaming and shouting and trying to hang on. But it's impossible. They tumble like toys into the churning sea.

With a great burst of steam, the *Lusitania* sinks. It gives one big last moan before going under. It's the most awful, heart-breaking sound you ever heard.

Your lifeboat overturns in the great downward surge of water. You look for something to hang onto. You see a suitcase and then a piece of wood. You grab for the wooden plank and hang onto it. It floats like a raft. You don't know how long you can hang on, though. Your shoulder was bruised when the lifeboat overturned. Now your arms are numb and aching.

All around you float pieces of debris from the ship. Boxes of cheese and tubs of butter float by. Canned goods bob in the water. It all seems so unbelievable. It's like a horrible nightmare.

You stare out across the water looking for rescue ships. Where are they? Surely they must know on shore what has happened. Why isn't the sea filled with rescue ships? You feel hopeless. You will surely die in this wild sea!

Your arms grow heavy. You must let go of the plank. Now you sink beneath the sea. Quarters of beef float by but you don't see them.

You drift westward on the tide. So many others are drifting with you. At dawn the next day over two hundred bodies wash up on the sands of Garretstown Strand. The people from the villages come down and help carry them to a morgue. You are one of the passengers who died in the sinking of the *Lusitania*.

■ *Turn to page 39.*

With a sick feeling, you leap from the lifeboat into the water. You swim madly away from the ship. Others are in the water too. A lot of debris floats around you. Pieces of smashed lifeboats bob nearby. Some bodies are floating too. You have never seen such horror. You are numb and sick. Suitcases and children's toys bump into your legs as you try to keep afloat.

You glance back to see the last seconds of the *Lusitania*. There is nothing but smoke now. At least you escaped the downward surge of water. Many did not. They were pulled to the bottom of the sea with the dying *Lusitania*.

But your arms ache and you are weary. You don't know how much longer you can swim. You spot a collapsible boat upside down in the water. You try to turn it right-side up and get in. You cannot do it. Sadly, desperately, you swim on.

Another collapsible boat with five people in it comes along. It's half full of water. Two women are bailing out water with their hands.

"Come on aboard," one of the women calls to you. "You look half drowned!" She hold out her hands and pulls you on board. But how can this miserable boat stay afloat? It's half sunk already!

You help with the rowing and the bailing. You don't say anything. You are too shocked and weak even to speak. You wonder why the rescue boats are not coming. The captain of the *Lusitania* must have radioed an S.O.S. the moment the torpedo hit. That was over an hour ago!

You are just twenty-five miles from land. Why doesn't help come?

"Are we going to die, Mommy?" a little girl asks her mother.

The mother holds the child close and doesn't answer.

Almost two hours pass. You are still bailing out water when you see a fishing boat. It's old.

"Help!" you all scream.

The fishing boat comes closer, and the sun-browned Irish fishermen pull you aboard. You are saved!

"Praise God," sobs the mother of the little girl.

The fishermen are very kind. They wrap you in blankets and give you hot drinks. You are so glad to be alive that tears run down your face.

■ *Turn to page 39.*

You climb from the crowded lifeboat and swim toward another boat with fewer passengers. But there's a big hole in it.

"We can't take more weight!" a man shouts.

You are caught up in the wild, choppy water. You turn to see the *Lusitania* going down. The dying ship is turning the whole sea into a whirlpool. Babies in wicker baskets with lifejackets around them are going down. You try to reach the babies. You must save them. But you can't. The wild water tosses a chunk of timber into your face. You gulp a mouthful of water. A terrible pain fills your head.

This is surely the end of you!

When you wake up you are on an old fishing schooner.

"We pulled you from the water," explains a kind-looking old Irish fisherman. "You were just about a goner."

You blink and look around. Then you remember the babies. "Did you save the babies?" you ask.

"What babies?" the mans asks. He shakes his head. "Oh, God have mercy. You mean there were babies in that wild sea? Ah, they should not have taken babies on a ship going into war waters."

"Oh," you groan, "there was a nursery full of babies on the *Lusitania*. I saw them in wicker baskets bobbing on the sea. . . ."

"Ah, what a pity," says the fisherman. Tears run down his craggy face.

You sit wrapped in a blanket as the fishing schooner takes you to shore. You feel very lucky to be alive. But you will never forget this tragedy as long as you live. You will always be wondering why it happened.

Why did a passenger ship go into waters where there was danger?

Why did the Germans torpedo a passenger ship?

Why did no rescue ships come to save all the drowning passengers? Only fishing schooners came.

You never learn the answers to your questions.

■ *Turn to page 39.*

You decide to trust the lifeboat. You help bail out water and hope and pray you are far enough from the dying *Lusitania*. When the great ship goes down, the wild water bounces you around. But you do not sink.

Your boat moves through the debris-filled water toward Queenstown.

"Why did the Germans torpedo the *Lusitania*?" you ask a grim sailor.

"I don't know. Maybe she was carrying ammunition for the war," he says.

"But the *Lusitania* was a passenger ship!" you cry. "They wouldn't have put ammunition on it."

"Don't know," the sailor says. "I saw boxes. Looked like shells. Didn't look like cheese or beef. But who knows?"

You look ahead at the shore. Queenstown is close now. You are going to be all right. You breathe a sigh of relief.

As you go ashore, everybody is quiet and sad. You find out that twelve hundred men, women, and children died on the *Lusitania*. You wonder why you were saved.

You attend the big funeral at the Queenstown cemetery on May 10, 1915. A hundred of the people who died on the *Lusitania* are buried in a large grave. The Americans are covered with American flags.

You cry at the funeral and try to figure out how this awful thing happened. Maybe you were a fool to take a holiday on a passenger ship going into war waters. But you are only a recent high school graduate. You are eighteen years old. Why didn't somebody tell you it wasn't safe? Why didn't somebody forbid civilians to travel on a ship if it wasn't safe?

And you wonder about what the sailor said. Did they hide ammunition on a passenger ship? Did the Germans know about that? Is that why they sent a torpedo into the side of the *Lusitania*? But how could any submarine commander send a torpedo into a passenger ship?

You never understand what happened. You sadly go home and try to get busy enough to forget. But as long as you live, you never forget the *Lusitania*.

■ *Turn to page 39.*

Bullets Below

When the *Lusitania* was sunk, a war was going on between Germany and England. Other nations were fighting too. It was World War I.

The *Lusitania* was not only carrying hundreds of civilians on a holiday. It was also carrying munitions (ammunition) for the war. It carried over twelve hundred boxes of shrapnel (shells that explode). It also carried about one hundred and seventy-three tons of cartridges (ammunition for guns). The passengers did not know this. They thought those boxes down below were only cheese and canned goods. Instead, they contained bullets for England.

Today the *Lusitania* lies three hundred feet down in the Atlantic Ocean twelve miles south of the Old Head of Kinsale (off the coast of Ireland). The sinking of the *Lusitania* was one of the saddest chapters of seagoing history.

Matching

1. The *Lusitania* was from this   a) Germany

   country: _____ .

2. This country torpedoed the *Lusitania:*   b) New York

   _____ .

3. Ammunition on the *Lusitania* included   c) Atlantic Ocean

   _____ .

4. Present location of the *Lusitania:*   d) England

   _____ .

5. The city the *Lusitania* sailed from: e) shrapnel

   _____ .

Group Activities

1. Using a large map, find the route of the *Lusitania* and notice where she was sunk. Also locate where battles were being fought at that time.

2. Discuss the following questions about the sinking of the *Lusitania*. Should a ship like the *Lusitania* have been allowed to take passengers into dangerous waters? Was it wrong to put ammunition on the ship?

3. As the *Lusitania* was getting ready to leave New York, the German government put a notice in the paper warning people not to sail on her. If you had tickets on the ship, would you have gone? The class should discuss this and vote to see if the majority would have gone or stayed home.

Individual Activities

1. The German lieutenant who fired the torpedo that hit the *Lusitania* saw all the people dying in the water. He only lived two more years after the incident. Then he died in another submarine. Do you think he was a bad person or only a good sailor? Write your opinion.

2. Find the painting of the *Sinking of the Lusitania* by Thomas M. Hemy. Write a paragraph about the scene. (The picture is on page 100 of *The Lusitania* by Colin Simpson.)

3. Many famous people died on the *Lusitania*. One was Elbert Hubbard, an American writer. Write a paragraph about him.

TRENCH WARFARE

It's 1918 and you are a young American soldier in France. World War I is raging all over Europe. Last summer you trained in North Carolina. It was hot and the training was hard. You were told war would be awful, but you never thought it would be this bad.

You are in a forest with a chill wind blowing. There are no trees in this forest. The trees have all been shot away in battles. The forest now looks like a black desert.

The snow piles high on your pack as you march. Your rifle is crusted with ice. You are temporarily separated from your group of soldiers. You will soon need shelter for the night.

"Look, there's a cottage," your buddy says.

You see a small stone cottage ahead. You rap on the door. A French woman opens up. "Ah," she says with a smile, *"les soldats Americains* [American soldiers]!" She lets you in quickly. The American soldiers have come to France to help the French in this war.

The French woman has three small children. They smile shyly at you. You are served thick, crusty bread and cheese. How good it tastes! It is so much better than your army rations of hardtack (hard coarse bread) and corned willy (salted beef). You had almost forgotten what real food tastes like!

The next morning you leave the cottage. You move toward the front (where the main battle is). You rejoin your group.

"We dig trenches, men!" shouts your sergeant.

You dig out a trench six feet deep. You will have to stand in this trench to keep from getting shot at by the enemy (the Germans). The Germans are digging a trench too. You have left about three hundred yards between the trenches. The land between the trenches is called "no man's land."

This is a dangerous place. When a soldier is caught here, he is easily shot. Even if you only poke your head out of your trench, you could get shot.

In a few days there will be a bitter battle. You will run from your trenches shooting. The Germans will do the same. Whoever wins will move ahead three hundred yards. That is how the war is being fought.

Your trench is two feet deep in water. You and twenty-four other men are packed in the small area. Water rats are swimming around your boots. What an awful place!

"Who wants sentry duty?" asks the sergeant. It's dangerous, but at least you can escape this foul trench for a little while!

■ *If you volunteer for sentry duty, turn to page 43.*

■ *If you stay in the trench, turn to page 44.*

Find out what your fate is!

41

"Me! I'll go!" you say. You must be out of this filthy trench. The smell of it is enough to kill someone!

You crawl out on your stomach. You inch along on the cold, gray mud. You are now crossing no man's land. It takes you about an hour to go a hundred and fifty yards. You keep your eyes wide open. You stare into the darkness until your eyes burn. If the Germans are getting ready to move out, you must spot the signs of it.

Suddenly you see the flash of a gun. You fire. Oh, no! It was just a flare. Now the Germans know you are out of your trench. They know where you are. They begin firing at you.

You crawl to a depression in the earth. It was made by a bomb exploding. But it won't give you much protection.

Should you run back toward the trench where your buddies are? Or should you run for the brick wall to your right? It was once the side of a farmer's cottage. Artillery smashed the cottage. But if you could make it to the wall, you'd be safe.

But wait! They have stopped firing at you. You lie motionless on the ground. Maybe they think you are dead. Your heart is beating wildly. You turn your head slightly. Are those dark shadows rising from the German trench? Are they coming to see if you are dead? No, the darkness is playing tricks on you!

You are turning numb. You can't lie motionless much longer. You must make a move. You raise your head a bit. It's closer to make the run to the brick wall. But you'd rather get back with your buddies.

You start moving slowly, not sure what direction to go in. As soon as your head is up a bit, a barrage of rifle fire streaks by. Luckily, it misses you. But you can't expect your luck to hold up much longer.

You must make a dash for it. You have darkness on your side now, but the dawn glows red in the sky.

■ *If you run back to the trench, turn to page 45.*

■ *If you run for the wall, turn to page 46.*

You decide to stay in the trench. At least you won't get your head shot off. You hope not, anyway. Sometimes enemy artillery rains down on the men in the trenches.

You remain in the trench for another day. Then orders come to advance. You climb from the trench and begin moving toward the enemy lines.

You are in the infantry. That's a tough place to be. But at least you don't have to go first. The field artillery goes first. They are supposed to batter the enemy. Then it's your turn to clean up. But as the field artillery advances, German machine gun bullets come thickly. You have never been so scared in your life. Growing up in your small town, you never dreamed you would ever be in such a place. You enjoyed detective stories. It was fun to read about your hero dodging bullets. But now you are dodging them. And it's no fun.

The roads are clogged with guns and trucks. Then you see a strange parade coming from the opposite direction. The walking wounded come with German prisoners. The wounded Americans are guarding the prisoners. But the prisoners are holding up the wounded. You stare at the faces of the men. They all look the same. The Germans are just boys. The Americans are just boys. Everybody looks like a tired schoolboy after a hard game.

By noon, you have captured the German trench. Now the whole army is advancing. The Germans are making a desperate stand. But you keep moving behind your firepower. You are afraid you are going to die in the next moment. You have to shoot two men. You try to forget what they looked like as they went down. You hope you don't see them in nightmares.

At the end of several days you are called a hero in the Battle of the Marne. You are just glad to be alive. You also survive the Battle of Argonne. And then Armistice Day comes. The war is over. You are going home.

Back home you have to decide what to do with your life. Should you go into the carpentry business like your father? Or should you learn to fly? Seeing those planes in the war got you interested in flying.

■ *If you become a carpenter, turn to page 47.*

■ *If you learn to fly, turn to page 48.*

You take off running for the trench. As the bullets fly around you, you drop, crawling and scrambling to safety. Somehow, you make it!

"I almost got killed!" you shout as you drop into the trench. Even the filthy, water-soaked trench looks good just now.

Your trench is supported by sandbags, poles, and sticks. The bottom is covered with boards, but they don't help much. They float in water much of the time.

Your bed at the end of the trench is a canvas cot. It's hard to sleep, though. Flies and mosquitoes breed in the water. And you are suffering from trench mouth. Your gums bleed and hurt. Your teeth seem about to fall from your mouth.

"I bet more fellows die of disease in these trenches than get shot," your buddy grumbles. It may be true! Living here sure makes you sick. And the big water rats swimming around don't help.

You don't think things can get any worse, but then they do. The Germans begin firing heavy artillery. Your best buddy falls at your side with a terrible wound in his head. You and another soldier keep him from falling into the water. You help bind his wound, but it's no use! The poor fellow is dead. And you have no time to grieve for him. You must grab your rifle and mount the firestep (where the soldiers stand to fire).

You blast away. Your whole body trembles as you fire. You want to get even for your dead buddy. Oh, sure, you know that German guy in the trench over there didn't have anything personal against your buddy. That German guy just fired. And your buddy got killed. That's the way war is.

You blast away. Pretty soon the other side is silent. "I guess I gave them a little something to think about," you say. You give your buddies an angry grin. You feel better.

And then another round of artillery comes from the German side. You are killed instantly. Over one hundred and sixteen thousand young Americans die in World War I. You are one of them.

■ *Turn to page 49.*

You race for the brick wall. Shells fall around you as you make your dash. You slip and fall, spraining your leg. You feel a hot, burning pain in your arm! You've been shot! You stumble again, then fall behind the wall. You sink into the gray, slimy mud. You must stop the blood spurting from your forearm. It's running down your sleeve.

You tie a rag around your arm and twist a stick in it. But you can't hold it. You are getting dizzy. Then everything turns black.

You never see your buddies who come to rescue you. You wake up in a field hospital. You have lost your arm just below the elbow. You are thankful to be alive, but it's a big shock to lose an arm. You are only twenty-one years old. What will you do without a right arm? What kind of job can you get?

When you get back to the United States, you can't be the carpenter you planned to be. Your father and your brothers are all carpenters. You planned to join the family business. Now you must do something else.

You get a job as a salesman. But it's not what you want. You used to like building houses. But it's no fun going from door to door selling vacuum cleaners.

You quit that job and get a new job selling sewing machines. You like that better. You learn a lot about the machines. You enjoy pointing out all the features to your customers. And, little by little, you grow to like selling. You drive all around the country. (You can drive using your left arm and your right stump.)

One day a small boy asks you how you lost your arm.

"In the war, son," you say.

"Oh boy! You're a hero," says the little boy. "Was it exciting?" He picks up a toy gun and shouts, "Bang!"

"War is not exciting. It's dirty and sad," you tell the boy. "It's standing in cold mud and being scared."

You sell the boy's mother a brand-new sewing machine. Then you give the boy a little toy flag. "I did my duty, son," you say. "It was the hardest thing I ever had to go through."

"Yes, sir," says the little boy. He waves as you drive away.

■ *Turn to page 49.*

You decide the war was enough excitement for a lifetime. You go into business with your father and brothers. Soon you are building rows of new homes in California. There's a building boom in California. Large country fields are turned into small lots. Small frame bungalows are put on each lot. They sell for one thousand dollars each.

You feel proud to be making homes for all those people. Why, you are building entire towns! You work in a place called San Clemente. You build homes with red tile roofs on the ocean shore. Then you go to Palm Springs in the desert and build stucco houses. You build some high-priced white, Spanish-style stucco houses with palm trees in the front yard.

As you finish each house, you get more money. You build your own house in an orange grove. Why, you are very comfortable now! You don't even think about the awful time you spent in the trenches during World War I. Then, in 1921, you get a phone call from the mother of an old buddy. You hadn't thought about Jack for a long time! He was at the Marne with you.

"My son is in the hospital," the mother says. "Would you visit him? He always talks about what good buddies you were. He really needs cheering up."

You knew Jack was gassed in the war. His back was hurt too. But you lost touch with him. You thought he was well by now. You thought he was busy making a new life as you are.

You get to the veterans' hospital the next week. You find poor Jack looking pale and thin. He never did recover from his war injuries. His back injury left him paralyzed. He has trouble breathing too.

You try to cheer up your old friend. You promise to come to see him often.

Jack was a young American soldier in France just like you. But he was unlucky. You came home okay. He came home a sick man. It could have been you. You leave the hospital and walk into the fresh air. You are young and healthy. But it could be you in Jack's bed just lying there.

You decide you will visit Jack every chance you get. He always liked to play checkers. Next time you'll bring a checkerboard.

■ *Turn to page 49.*

Your father thinks you are out of your mind. But you can't forget those planes darting through the sky. You admired those daring aviators in the war. They seemed like a wonderful bunch of guys. You must find out what it feels like to fly.

You look up an old army buddy who was an aviator in the war. He tells you about a little flying school in Florida. You scrape up the money to go there.

After you learn to fly, you love it. You feel like an eagle soaring through the sky. You begin to go to the air races in St. Louis. You meet other daring young pilots. You even enter one of the races. You don't win anything, but it's a big thrill being in the race.

"I could never be a carpenter now, Pa," you tell your father.

"But flying planes is a hobby, son," he argues. "You have to make a living."

"And besides," your mother adds, "it's dangerous! If we were meant to fly, God would have given us wings!"

You look for ways to make money flying. You ask your old army buddy.

"Airmail, old bean," the fellow says. "Fly for the Post Office. The money is great."

"Yeah!" you shout. "People can send letters airmail. Somebody has to deliver them."

You have to wait a while before you are hired as an airmail pilot. But you finally get the job. It pays one thousand dollars a month. Why, that's a fortune! Most fellows are making only a couple of hundred a month!

But there are dangers in your new job. When the weather is bad, those little planes can crash. But your luck holds up. You keep on flying and making good money. You make friends with famous men like Wiley Post and Howard Hughes.

You never get over your love for flying. Even after you stop flying for the Post Office, you fly for fun. On a bright, sunny day, you just have to be soaring like a bird!

■ *Turn to page 49.*

The Red Cross

In 1881, a former schoolteacher named Clara Barton saw soldiers who had been wounded in the Civil War. Their suffering touched her heart. She thought there should be an organization to help people like that. So she set up the American Red Cross.

In World War I, the Red Cross staffed almost sixty field hospitals in the battle areas. They ran forty-seven ambulance companies. To the suffering wounded, the Red Cross was a welcome sign. The ambulance with the red cross on it could drive through enemy lines. Everybody knew these were people helping the helpless.

Twenty thousand nurses served in the Red Cross during World War I. Hundreds of others ran canteens (places where soldiers could get food and drink). In a terrible war with much suffering, the Red Cross was the hand of comfort.

True/False

_____ 1. The Americans in World War I fought on the German side.

_____ 2. Clara Barton founded the American Red Cross.

_____ 3. Trenches were common on both sides in World War I.

_____ 4. The land betwen the trenches was called "no man's land."

_____ 5. Hardtacks were the hard army cots the soldiers slept on.

Group Activities

1. Using a map of Europe, find the following places where American service people fought battles in World War I.
   Cantigny   Meuse-Argonne   Saint-Mihiel
   Chateau-Thierry   Soissons   Belleau Wood

2. Discuss the life of a World War I soldier. Which hardships do you think were the worst?

3. Find some songs made famous during World War I. Play them, and then discuss them. "Over There," "I Didn't Raise My Boy to Be a Soldier," "Roses of Picardy," and "My Buddy" are a few of them.

Individual Activites

1. Write one paragraph about one of the following personalities of the World War I era:
   Woodrow Wilson   General John Pershing   Eddie Rickenbacker   Joyce Kilmer

2. Imagine you are a soldier in World War I. Write a letter home about the trenches.

3. Many young poets died in World War I. One was the talented Joyce Kilmer. Find some poems by Kilmer and read them. His poem "Trees" became world-famous.

Answer Key

1. **Ellis Island Decision**

   1. T   4. F
   2. T   5. T
   3. F

2. **Muckrakers Wanted**

   1. c   4. e
   2. a   5. d
   3. b

3. **Getting the Vote**

   1. b   4. e
   2. a   5. c
   3. d

4. **A Fateful Voyage**

   1. d   4. c
   2. a   5. b
   3. e

5. **Trench Warfare**

   1. F   4. T
   2. T   5. F
   3. T

Bibliography

1. Ellis Island Decision   Link, Arthur S. *American Epoch.* Knopf, 1963 (p. 57).

Mann, Arthur. *Immigrants in American Life.* Houghton Mifflin, 1968 (pp. 28, 71–75, 86, 90).

Severn, Bill. *Ellis Island.* Julian Messner, 1971.

2. Muckrakers Wanted   Current, Richard N., and John A. Garraty, eds. *Words That Made American History.* Little Brown, 1963 (pp. 168, 189).

Glaab, Charles N. *The American City.* Dorsey Press, 1963 (pp. 337, 344).

Wish, Harvey. *Contemporary America.* Harpers, 1961 (pp. 73–75).

3. Getting the Vote   Scott, Anne Firor. *Women in American Life.* Houghton Mifflin, 1970 (pp. 101–10).

200 Years: A Bicentennial Illustrated History of the United States. U.S. News and World Report, 1973 (pp. 88–89).

4. A Fateful Voyage   Simpson, Colin. *The Lusitania.* Little Brown, 1972.

5. Trench Warfare   *America, A Library of Original Sources.* Vol. XII. VFW, 1925 (pp. 101–16).

200 Years: A Bicentennial Illustrated History of the United States. U.S. News and World Report, 1973 (pp. 122–29).

"World War I," *The World Book Year Book,* 1987 (pp. 535–36).